Equally Yoked:
TRUST IN RELATIONSHIPS
FOR SPIRITUAL WELLNESS

Veronica Fallah
Owner, Venerate Care, LLC
Pastoral Care Pastor at
PowerShift Worship Center Christian Church
Local Hospital Chaplain

Purpose Publishing
1503 Main Street #168 ❧ Grandview, Missouri
www.purposepublishing.com

ISBN: 978-0-6928942-2-4

Editing by Felicia Murrell
Book Cover Design by PP Team of Designers

For permission and requests,
write to the publisher:
1503 Main Street, #168, Grandview, MO 64030.

Author Inquiries may be sent to
chaplainveronica03@gmail.com
www.VeronicaFallah.com
www.veneratecare.com

Table of Contents

DEDICATION

This book is dedicated to my parents A. D. and Dorothy Moss, who always believed in me when I did not believe in myself. You two exemplify what it means to trust God in a lifetime commitment of holy matrimony.

To my husband, with much appreciation and love, I am so grateful to God for your agreement to walk together with me.

To my daughters, Ashley and LaTecia Posey and my grandchildren; you all know you give me life.

FOREWORD
Equally Yoked

My grandmother used to say to me, "Birds of a feather flock together." I often wondered what that meant. Though the meaning became clear when I befriended schoolmates who didn't match my family's expectations of similar background, race, or religion. There was a palatable worry that I would get in with the "wrong crowd" and be hurt. Or worse, that I would enter another culture and be *lost to them.*

Over the generations, Christian parents and grandparents have hoped their children would select spouses whose language, looks, and religion would easily fit in with familiar family patterns, thus avoiding discomfort and stress not only for the married couple but for other relatives, as well. The words of St. Paul provide the perfect biblical injunction: "Do not be unequally yoked together with unbelievers. For what do righteousness and wickedness have in common" (2 Corinthians 6:14)?

Her family and her church taught Veronica Fallah this same idea: *Dear, make sure you select a marriage partner with whom you will be equally yoked.* She, along with many of us, believed it and followed it. But like so many rules out of context or without nuance, she has seen and experienced the suffering caused when Paul's words are used as a blanket formula.

Veronica Fallah's timely work invites us to look deeper at Paul's plowing metaphor to find not only how it has sometimes been misapplied, but also to explore its depth so that we might claim it today for the wisdom it has to offer. The work of pulling a plow is less when two oxen share equally; but if one does most of the work, it can become overstrained, and the wooden yoke can chafe the shoulders raw. Paul and grandmothers alike are aware that power dynamics are at play in marriages and other relationships, and that to partner with someone not of one's faith or type can—and often has—led to heavy burden-bearing by the faithful partner, or worse, their loss of connection to a life-giving faith community.

But in this diverse world, as Fallah demonstrates, we are called upon to know, love, and work beside all kinds of people who differ from us in ways beyond our imagining: background, language, age, education level, experience of the Holy, hope for the future, even ability (or not) to converse with strangers. To have intimate relationships, to make a difference in the world, to follow our bliss, or even to live out our faith requires that we share our bird feeders with wrens and blue jays and cardinals and chickadees. We find ourselves invited to pull our burdens together with all manner of people God sends to be with us. This may require us to find ways to make yokes that accommodate the short and the tall, the broad-shouldered and slight-shouldered, those who move on foot and those who push themselves on wheels.

Pastor Fallah knows this at the depth of her being from both perspectives. First, she suffered a divorce from someone of very similar background whom family and church would have agreed was a husband who would be equally yoked with her. Then, sometime later, she met a man utterly her opposite. He was from a different country, different culture, and different religion — a religion with scripture in which being "unequally yoked" was not mentioned as a problem.

I was privileged to witness her struggle to be faithful to her God, as revealed in scripture, but also in tradition, experience, and reason. As her seminary faculty advisor at St. Paul School of Theology, I overheard her discussion with herself and her God. Eventually, she truly felt God calling her and Kia to marry, especially sustained by his commitment to support her in her work as a pastor, in her spiritual life, and in her relationship with her God. He, too, was willing to be honest about his own commitments, beliefs, concerns, and hopes. They each agreed to find individual supports as well as to support and be nourished by each other.

I was honored to conduct their service of holy matrimony, which (in my tradition) required that I work with them on premarital counseling. I shall never forget the thoughtful, sometimes tearful, always respectful conversations about their differences and the likely stress-points they might face. I found them practical ("Here's how we plan to celebrate Christmas"), and always open, in wonder, to the unexpected and surprises they expected to encounter day by day. It has not always been easy. But it has always been loving and adventuresome, with deep listening and honoring, working together with much hospitality and laughter. Their joy is godly and I am in awe of them.

Out of her own rich experience as well as her theological reflection, Pastor Fallah invites us to address the question: *How can we imagine "equal" yoking with people who may not look nor act like us?* In *Equally Yoked*, she reminds us that God made all these different kinds of people and wants us to be in community together, including playing and working together, dancing and bearing each other's burdens. I found myself recalling the core biblical message that insists we be willing to be paired with an abundance of partners of God's choice, for love of us and each other: "have life... abundantly"(John 10:10b), "walk in love, as Christ loved us, and gave himself for us" (Ephesians 5:2), be "the light of the world" (Mt. 5:14). The greatest gift is that the Lord blesses us, keep us, and give us peace (Numbers 6:24-26). Because God blesses us, we should "love the stranger as ourselves" (Lev. 19:34). Jesus' whole sermon on the mount (Mt. 5-7) points to a spiritual relationship of loving openness to God so that we can love one another as Christ loved us (John 13:34, 15:12). And Christ loved everyone, including strangers (Luke 10:29-37), even enemies.

Fallah witnesses to this core biblical message by sharing her own experience that when God joins us together, it is *God's Spirit* who shows us what the newly-shaped yoke will look like so that we can be spiritually connected in community. She urges us: "We must learn to trust God's Spirit within while

We must learn to trust God's spirit within while building trusting relationships with each other.

building trusting relationships with each other"(chapter 2). Fallah's own prayer practice undergirds this exhortation. The Spirit will guide us in discerning relationships and in using our gifts and talents for building up the very diverse family of faith and the human family. This life of trust and exercising our gifts in relationship gives our life joy, meaning and purpose. It makes us spiritually whole and well.

Pastor Fallah's own call is to help others find *spiritual wellness,* which is part of the work of *SALVATION.* The Latin root — *salve* — refers to health, healing, wholeness, and wellness. How do we become spiritually well? Trust the Spirit. Set up practices: Be in prayer. Fast. Listen. Use your gifts. And be "yoked in the word of God," the scripture. She reveals how we can use scripture to lean into trust and practice this healing wellness.

Pastor Fallah then reveals a rich creativity of faithful relationships in our *families* (chapters 5-6), *friendships* (chapter 7), *vocations* (chapter 8) and *faith communities* (chapter 9). The very questions she poses expand the meaning of "equally-yoked" to vibrant contemporary interpretations ("Is your family equally yoked? In every area of life does your family have a strong structure of support? What does your family agreement look like with your immediate and extended family?").

She concludes with a profound insight: "*I yoked myself with the strength within.*" How many of us consider God to be our yoking-partner? Yet doesn't Jesus say, "I have called you friends" (John 15:15)? With the authority of a pastor who has a deep redeeming partnership with God, the author claims a hidden truth: the Spirit of God is our primary yoking partner. For we humans are *spiritual beings.* It is Christ's Spirit who strengthens us and enables differing partners to pull equally for the love of God and neighbor.

Pastor Fallah has been passionately teaching, inviting, and enabling her parishioners, colleagues, and friends to be spiritually well for decades. She has seen the spiritual dis-ease of persons unable to draw upon the loving kindness and strength of their God in dire times. Wholeness and healing are available to us if, in faith and confidence, we pull together, allowing God's Spirit to connect with us and yoke us with the others *God* chooses for us. The Holy Spirit is the strength within us. Even people of faith do not always expect, ask, pursue or even notice God's presence, even when it's right there with us. For those people of faith and for those who aren't sure they have any faith, this book offers spiritual healing. Our goal is not just to follow some external set of rules—such as "marry someone just like ourselves." Rather, we are to

11

use the free will God gave us to *agree to walk together* (Amos 3:3) in relationship even when it's hard. We were made for community. As Veronica Fallah says, "God has called us to share, belong, serve, and suffer together" (chapter 9).

It is my hope that this book will bless you as it has blessed me, inspiring readers to be intentionally open and desirous of Holy Presence, Holy Wholeness, and Holy Relationship. May you be inspired to become aware of the Gift in the particular people God sends to love and work with you and to create yokes for sharing the burden. And most of all, may you follow the author's courage in allowing the Holy Spirit to be your primary yoke-partner. May the ease of the Divine Yoke (Matthew 11:30) open the way for your *wellness* – your *salvation* – in all your work and grant you and yours weekly joy at Sabbath rest and stillness in the intimacy of your hearts.

Epiphany, 2017

The Rev. Susan Marie Smith, Ph.D.
(The Rev.) Susan Marie Smith, Ph.D.
Ammasusan.smith@gmail.com
CHURCH: Episcopal Church of the Nativity
7300 Lantern Road, Indianapolis, 46256

Introduction

As I embrace this path of writing wrapped with biblical scriptures on *Equally Yoked: Trust in Relationships For Spiritual Wellness,* my prayer for you is to own your truth and recognize those relationships in which you agree to connect throughout your life. By believing in God's Spirit as the only validation for relationships we agree to walk together.

This book has been in the works for quite sometime. With the encouragement of my spouse, parents, and a dear friend, colleague and pastor, Yolanda Roseby, I started writing what God has placed in my mind and spirit.

What is it that brings us to an agreement with another person? Are our expectations, spoken and unspoken, made clear in our agreements to walk together? Journey with me on the development of being "equally yoked" and embrace the trust and relationships God gives you for spiritual wellness.

The scriptures of focus are 2 Corinthians 6:14, "Do not be unequally yoked together with unbelievers: for what fellowship has righteousness with unrighteousness? And what communion has light with darkness?" and Amos 3:3, "Will two people walk together unless they have agreed to do so?"

Throughout the book, I will explain what led me to the phrase, "equally yoked" and I will share personal experiences about relationships I have had. The chapters within describe my relationships with God; spouse; family; friends; vocations; and community of faith, as well as connect with biblical texts on trust and relationships.

What is it that brings us to an agreement with another person? Are our expectations, spoken and unspoken, made clear in our agreements to walk together? Journey with me on the development of being "equally yoked" and embrace the trust and relationships God gives you for spiritual wellness.

Before we move forward let us define what the terms equally yoked and spiritual wellness mean in this book. Matthew 11:28-30 (NKJV) explains what is meant in being equally yoked. The passage shows Jesus with His arms open reaching out toward you, saying, "Come to Me, all *you* who labor and are heavy laden, and I will give you rest. Take My yoke upon you and learn from Me, for I am gentle and lowly in heart, and you will find rest for your souls. For My yoke *is* easy and My burden is light."

Yoke is used of something that represents a bond between two parties. Jesus's bond of giving us rest for our labor is His agreement when we come to Him. So in this book, equally yoked is described as two people joined, linked, or united in a close relationship in an agreement of support, respect, and empowerment for growth. Spiritual wellness involves seeking meaning and purpose for our lives while allowing our beliefs and values to guide our decisions and actions. When we are able to live fully by our beliefs and values, it will show in our actions. Then we are connecting to what is called spiritual wellness.

Chapter One:
The Conversation

While exploring the possibilities of writing this book, I mentioned my vision to my parents. I talked with my mom daily and during one of our conversations I told her the name of the book. I started outlining to her what I hoped to accomplish by writing. When she heard the name of the book, she asked me about various relationships and questioned if all of my relationships had been equally yoked? I gave her my answer, which will become clear to you as you embrace each chapter of this book.

One day I shared some concerns about a work relationship with my father. Speaking of humankind in general, he immediately replied, "TRUST NO MAN." I paused. My father shared in depth his faith beliefs on how the Bible tells believers to "not trust in man," (Psalm 118:8). I understood his reply as well as the biblical writings. However, I know we must have some level of trust when we enter into relationships especially if we are to be equally yoked. There indeed is a trust factor in being equally yoked and we must trust the Spirit of God to connect to that place of wellness.

I have learned that in relationships there should be some type of understanding of expectations and goals set by each person. This must happen in order for the relationship to move forward in accomplishing the expectations and goals that have been set. Something to think about as you continue to read: Do those in the relationship trust one another with the spoken and unspoken goals set and are their expectations communicated openly?

Let us look closely at some of the texts in the Bible that talk about trust and relationships. First, we will review Amos 3:3, "Will two people walk together unless they have agreed to do so?" In relationships, we must know and understand the expectations of the other to minimize conflict and hardship.

Second, let us review Deuteronomy 22:10, "Do not plow with an ox and a donkey together." This scripture says that two working together must be of the same breed and/or size to balance the load. Biblical scholar John Gill wrote of this passage, "They might be used separately, but not together; nor was it uncommon in some countries for donkeys to be employed in plowing as well as oxen . . . mystery of this is, that godly and ungodly persons are not to be yoked together in religious fellowship."[i]

We must look deeper than religious fellowship as the scholar penned. In every relationship there must be an even balance in carrying the load. We must be in agreement with the other person to work together equally in "plowing the field" that is before us. In our minds, we may be stuck on the ending of Gill's writing, "godly and ungodly" which leads me to our third scripture to explore. "Do not be unequally yoked together with unbelievers: for what fellowship has righteousness with unrighteousness? And what communion has light with darkness" (2 Corinthians 6:14)? I would like for us to think about this scripture let it formulate our thoughts and put into words what is developing within us as we read this book.

I pray that you will connect to the trust in relationships for being spiritually well in your own relationships. Sometimes, when hearing the text, "Do not be unequally yoked together," we judge what is godly and ungodly without getting to know the situation. Second Corinthians 6:14 is a foundational text for people who are getting married. Many clergy leaders asked couples, "Are you two equally yoked?" And in many Christian traditions, the clergy may inquire if the couple belongs to the same faith denomination. Most couples entering a marriage are looking for a helpmeet to deal with everyday life situations, not a hindrance. They are connecting with someone to support him or her along the course of building a life together.

We look for the same thing in building trust and relationships in our friendships and families. In my pursuit, I am looking at relationships between ourselves, others, and God. In any relationship, yoked people are on the same path. When we connect in relationships we are not looking to connect with someone who might hinder us in the plan that is set before us which is to become who we are created to be. We are looking for support. These two texts, 2 Corinthians 6:14 and Deuteronomy 22:10 highlight "clean and unclean" and "godly and ungodly." I would like for you to think about and identify the types of relationships you have encountered and experienced that have helped you understand if your relationships are equally yoked.

Use the journal lines on the next two pages to answer the following question.

How would you approach a conversation on being equally yoked?

_____

_____

_____

_____

_____

_____

_____

_____

_____

_____

_____

_____

Chapter Two:
Trusting In A World Of Differences

"We become not a melting pot but a beautiful mosaic: Different people, different beliefs, different yearnings, different hopes, and different dreams."[ii]

The above quote paints a picture of differences within our lives. Our world is made up of different things that bring in the beauty of all of God's designs. With all the differences in our world, and the differences we face in life, what is God saying to our spirits about being yoked in the plan that God designed for each of us? We must learn to trust God's spirit within while building trusting relationships with each other.

We can find the answer to our questions about being equally yoked when we consciously seek the plan God has designed for us. When we earnestly seek God, we will not allow traditional doctrine to rule our direction in a negative way. We will embrace biblical writings in a way that leads to wellness. We seek God for a relevant understanding of God's word today. We strive to intentionally seek a true relationship with God, others, and ourselves in our world of differences. By studying biblical writings we are enabled to live full lives. We do this by trusting in one another's gifts and talents that keep us yoked in the word of God in all relationships.

What is this trust? In the introduction, you may remember the statement by my father, "Trust No Man!" I get what my dad was saying to me. He had experienced much disappointment throughout his life and he believed that if it were not for his faith in God, his life would have been impossible to bear. However, we must have some level of trust with the people God has allowed us to build relationships with. I believe my full trust has to be in the Lord, as my father stated. Our trust in the Lord guides us to trust in others whom God has us to engage with in our everyday lives. God's system is to apply life-giving strength to one another so we might live in a realm of fullness of love, power, and a sound mind; a realm of no lack, by trusting the discernment we have within. The world's system is to do things without direction from the Spirit of God and to live in fear while looking out for yourself and to avoid embracing this wonderful world of differences.

"Trust in the Lord with all your heart; don't rely on your own intelligence. Know God in all your paths and God will keep your ways straight," (Proverbs 3:5-6, Common English Bible). This text clearly states our trust should be in God alone and not our own knowledge. We should keep full trust in our Creator. In our world's system, we find ourselves dealing with differences and obstacles almost daily. In some cases, people may fall into the trap of trusting the world's system instead of God's system.

Several years ago, I attended a training seminar sponsored by Christian Church the Disciples of Christ on Pro-Reconciliation Anti-Racism in the Greater Kansas City region. The speaker made a statement about the system of our nation. It was stated that our system has established racism, developing a clear line of separating the whites and blacks that allowed many minds in our nation to live in the fear of equality and equity. Can we trust our world system? Babies are color blind and children are honest and innocent from the heart. During a period of segregation in the United States in the late 1950s, a little Southern white girl noticed a water fountain with the words COLORED ONLY above it. She was excited and preceded to drink from the fountain. Her mom scolded her telling her to never ever drink from the COLORED fountain. The little girl was confused and felt she and her mom were missing an opportunity to drink color water. She wanted to see blue, green and red colors from the fountain.[iii] This little girl did not have any idea that the fountain was in place for a race of people. Her innocence of wanting the colored water demonstrates that segregation is learned in the American system. We must remember our trust should be in God's system and not in the world's system.

In 2014, several World and National news features may have caused some to put their trust in the world's system rather than God's system. Below are some of the breaking news stories on one local news station:

- *Ebola Crisis* — there is possible plans to deploy 3,000 U.S. military troops to West Africa.
- *Home Depot* management says after the breach there are 56 million cards at risk. If you used your bankcard at Home Depot between April 2014 and September 2014, you need to change your card number.
- *ISIS Terror* — should President Obama put boots on the ground on Syrian soil?
- *Local schools* are on lockdown — possible bomb threat.

In hearing these news stories, we may have had cause to fear for our health (Ebola), our finances (bankcards breached), or our protection (possible war/bomb threat).

What is happening in our own lives? Are we trusting and focusing on God's system, the world's system, or our own system? God is calling us to put our full TRUST in God's system and not our own system or this world's system. Is it a struggle for us to fully trust the Lord? When we put our trust in God, we can find peace to live in a way that gives us meaning and purpose in our lives, which is being yoked by God's Spirit for spiritual wellness.

We may desire to put our full trust in God's plan, and yet find ourselves at a standstill in fully trusting with our minds and hearts. In order to get started, we must learn to apply scripture so that our hearts and minds are aligned to TRUST the spiritual path that yokes us to become spiritually well. I am not saying this trust for spiritual wellness is an easy path. We are going to face some rough roads, but we need not be afraid.

"Do not fret because of those who are evil or be envious of those who do wrong; for like the grass they will soon wither, like green plants they will soon die away. **Trust** in the Lord and do well; dwell in the land and enjoy safe pasture. Take delight in the Lord, and the Lord will give you the desires of your heart. Commit your way to the Lord; trust in God and God will do this; God will make your righteous reward shine like the dawn, your vindication like the noonday sun. **Be still** before the Lord and **wait patiently** for God; do not fret when people succeed in their ways, when they carry out their wicked schemes. Refrain from anger and turn from wrath; do not fret it leads only to evil. For those who are evil will be destroyed, but those who **hope** in the Lord will inherit the land" (Psalm 37:1-9, New International Version).

Faced with challenges, I have thought about how I should handle these situations. I would start mapping out plans of action. God's words in this Psalm of David helped me with trusting God's spiritual path for my life by learning how to be still and wait patiently in the hope of receiving what God was doing in my life, continuing to live in spiritual wellness. When I release my challenges to God's plan, my life is so much lighter. I do not feel like I needed to take matters into my own hands. This trust can bring forth healing.

God gives us reassurance of His power in our lives. We must "let go and let God" to handle situations by trusting with our whole hearts and minds. We should not take matters into our own hands. "The simple message is to maintain patience in the midst of troubles.

God's people can have such patience because they know their eternal reward will abundantly surpass any temporal troubles."[iv] When we commit our ways to the Lord, the Lord will elevate us to new heights. This elevation happens when we focus on God's plan that is a life of right living and not taking matters into our own hands. This elevation also comes by trusting the plan God has for us. When we face heartaches and disappointments, God's hands of protection are there to cover us.

One day, while going through my news feed on Facebook, I clicked on a video of comedienne Sheryl Underwood. She shared how she had been badmouthed by a group of her peers called the Queens of Comedy. After hearing how they truly felt about her appearance and ability, Sheryl stated that she was bruised but not broken. She chose not to confront them, but reflected on the comments and used her pain for gain in her life. She believes hearing those comments made by this group of comediennes helped her become the success she is today. She is currently on the television show, "The Talk" and performs standup shows around the country.

We should be able to hear hurtful things about ourselves and trust the path by holding onto the peace of God. Can we be still, wait patiently and trust in God with our hearts and minds so that we can live the lives God has designed for us? In relationships, do you believe one must have some level of trust? What does trust in a relationship mean to you? This would be a good time to reflect over our lives to see if there are areas where we need to trust God more in becoming yoked in our relationships toward spiritual wellness. Healing is just ahead and it starts within. Let us ready ourselves to fully trust God's plan for a journey of being equally yoked with others, as we trust God in each relationship.

Use the journal lines on the next two pages to answer the following question.

What systems are you trusting?

_____

_____

_____

_____

_____

_____

_____

_____

_____

_____

_____

_____

Chapter Three:
Having Self-Worth For Ourselves

In thinking about owning what brings value and meaning to our lives, how do we stay connected to a relationship of self-worth? What does it mean to have a relationship with one's self? I am referring to a person who truly knows their self-worth and lives accordingly towards being spiritually well.

As Christians, some of us have the determination to live well, grow and serve throughout our faith journeys. Some of us choose to attend worship services while others may choose to find quiet time in sacred places to equip ourselves and to know our self-worth.

In the book of Esther, we read about two queens who knew their self-worth, Queen Vashti and Queen Esther.

The biblical story begins at the end of a feast given by King Ahasuerus:

"In the third year of his reign, he gave a banquet for all his officials and ministers. The army of Persia and Media and the nobles and governors of the provinces were present, (A seven day banquet with guest including leading men in the

*province)....Furthermore, Queen Vashti gave a
banquet for the women in the palace of King
Ahasuerus" (Esther 1:3,9).*

The women were in a separate area and the
king summoned his wife to the feast simply to
show off her beauty. Had the king been sober,
he would not have considered such a breach of
custom. He knew that Eastern women lived in
seclusion and that such a request as he made in
his drunken state amounted to a gross insult.
For Vashti to appear in the banquet hall, even
dressed in her royal robes and crown, would
have been as degrading as having a woman of
our modern world go naked into a man's
party. According to the scripture that follows,
Queen Vashti did not comply with the King's
request.

*"According to the law, what is to be done to Queen
Vashti because she has not performed the command
of King Ahasuerus conveyed by those closest to the
King....For this deed of the queen will be made
known to all women, causing them to look with
contempt on their husbands, since they will say,
"King Ahasuerus commanded Queen Vashti to be
brought before him, and she did not come." This
very day the noble ladies of Persia and Media who
have heard of the queen's behavior will rebel against
the king's officials, and there will be no end of
contempt and wrath! If it pleases the king, let a*

royal order go out from him, and let it be written
among the laws of the Persians and the Medes so
that it may not be altered, that Vashti is never again
to come before King Ahasuerus; and let the king
give her royal position to another who is better than
she. So when the decree made by the king is
proclaimed throughout all his kingdom, vast as it is,
all women will give honor to their husbands, high
and low alike" (Esther 1: 15, 17-20).

Vashti knew her value and despite the circumstance, she stood on her self-knowledge of what was right for her. She was dethroned, but she knew her worth. Her stand opened a door for God's protection for a nation. When we embrace the strength within to stand on our core values, it leads to a path for healing not just for us, but healing for others as well. This story continues with the king meeting Esther. Esther also stood on her self-worth.

"The king loved Esther more than all the other
women; of all the virgins she won his favor and
devotion, so that he set the royal crown on her head
and made her queen instead of Vashti" (Esther
2:17).

When a law was set with the seal of the king's ring, it was not to be broken. Esther had a relative named Mordecai. Mordecai had an enemy named Haman, who had a law in place to eliminate all Jews and the law prevented the Jews from defending themselves.

> *"Mordecai told them to reply to Esther, 'Do not think that in the king's palace you will escape any more than all the other Jews. For if you keep silence at such a time as this, relief and deliverance will rise for the Jews from another quarter, but you and your father's family will perish. Who knows? Perhaps you have come to royal dignity for just such a time as this.' Then Esther said in reply to Mordecai, Go, gather all the Jews to be found in Susa, and hold a fast on my behalf, and neither eat nor drink for three days, night or day. My maids and I will also fast as you do. After that I will go to the king, though it is against the law; and if I perish, I perish" (Esther 4:13-16).*

Esther knew there was a possibility of her death in going to the king without being summoned. The combination of Mordecai's wisdom and Esther's courage became the means of lightening the load of the Jews under Persian rule. There was a need for the oppressed to act shrewdly and boldly for justice to prevail.

God brought Esther to the throne for such a time. God's protection is vivid in this world. God will protect us from the hands of our enemies, just as God protected Mordecai and the Jewish people from Haman's hand.

Let's look closer at the two women in the book of Esther. At different points in the story, the leading characters resembled each other directly or in reverse. The disobedient Queen Vashti was deposed, but Esther, the new queen who replaced her, triumphantly defied the law. Esther successfully begged the king for the lives of her people whom Haman had doomed. Vashti was a "Persian queen, a woman of clear judgment of magnificent self-control and capable of the noblest self-sacrifice. Vashti is known as the woman who exalted modesty."[v]

Esther was chosen to succeed Vashti. The woman who saved her nation from genocide was an orphan who was raised by her relative Mordecai. Both women exhibited self-reverence, self-recognition, self-knowledge and self-control that are attributes leading to being spiritually well.

Can you identify with Vashti or Esther? Have you ever heard the voice of God calling for self-recognition, self-knowledge, self-control, and for you to exhibit self–reverence? Knowing your self-worth will lead you to a path never walked before, a path of being yoked within for wholeness to live as your true self.

In the sight of God, we are kings and queens. By God's grace, we come to know our self-worth then others can recognize it. God calls us to be set apart from that which the world is doing. God will give us self-knowledge and self-control. Esther's stand for purity and being true to God in living her life in full alignment to a path of spiritual wellness, yoked her in a service of embracing courage, which led to her obedience in saving a nation.

The common goals for us as believers are to love, serve, and obey. By loving, serving, and obeying, we can empower ourselves during our spiritual journey in being yoked in God's will for owning our self-worth. How are we going to keep and enhance our self-worth while seeking the path of being spiritually yoked while daily living out our values and beliefs? When we truly live within our values and beliefs, we are living spiritually well.

Use the journal lines on the next two pages to answer the following question.

How do you connect to your self-worth?

Veronica Fallah

Chapter Four:
God, Our Faith Creator

How do we as believers connect to God's plan for us in an equally yoked relationship? Can we be equally yoked with God? The best way to be completely yoked in the plan God has for our lives is by loving, serving, and obeying the Spirit of God within, which leads us to our fullest potential in everyday life.

In the Bible, we find many scriptures that outline how we should connect to the Spirit of God. In Paul's letter to the Corinthians (1 Corinthians 2:4-5) he states, "My message and my preaching were not with wise and persuasive words, but with a demonstration of the Spirit's power, so that your faith might not rest on human wisdom, but on God's power. However, as it is written: "What no eye has seen, what no ear has heard, and what no human mind has conceived" — the things God has prepared for those who love him."[vi] The things God has prepared for us come to life when our faith is developed by God's Spirit. Our faith increases when we experience God's presence moving in our lives. Do we depend on God's Spirit, our minds, or others? The Apostle Paul shows us that he was very aware of his limitations when he shared the message of the gospel. He knew the emotion of the mind affects the body.

Paul relied on God's Spirit to convey the message of Jesus Christ to the people in Corinth. In this setting, the Greeks were impressed by enticing and eloquent speeches. However, Paul expressed that change comes only through divine power not enticing words. We cannot trust in our own strength or our own minds. God's Spirit leads us on a path of being yoked with God and this leads us to spiritual wellness. God will meet us where we are if we are willing to follow. God has secured our salvation when we take time to fortify our faith through the gospel and apply the principles that strengthen our faith.

Faith is fortified through exercising our beliefs. To hear the plans for our lives, I believe we must take time to read the scriptures, pray, and fast. I have witnessed God's Spirit moving in my life. I can recall a time waiting over nine months on an answer for tickets needed for travel. God's Spirit compelled me to fast and pray and within twenty-four hours of my fasting and praying, I received tickets in the mail for my travel. Another time, I remember feeling very lonely and wanted to hear from a close companion who was deployed overseas. I began praying and seeking God through the word of God. That night I prayed in the spirit and within the hour my phone rang and I was able to engage in a loving conversation with the companion who had been in my heart.

Paul referenced Isaiah 64:4, "Since ancient times no one has heard, no ear has perceived, no eye has seen any God besides you, who acts on behalf of those who wait for him." The book of Isaiah describes the blessedness of those who were admitted to the divine favor. It also tells about those who had communion with God and those to whom God manifested Himself as their friend.

Paul used it to denote the happiness that would result from communication of the divine favor to the soul. Paul was not referring to the happiness of heaven as in Isaiah. He was referring to the happiness of God revealing the things to Christians by God's Spirit. Through developing our faith, we can see the things God has prepared for us by the wisdom that is made known to the people of God.

If we are deaf to the word of God, God's secrets will not be made known to us. Paul's preaching included how the Holy Spirit opens hearts and minds and convinces us of our need to be in right relationship with God through faith in the risen Christ. In being in right relationship with God, our lives are transformed and we receive spiritual purity, wholeness, and purpose for our lives. When we take time in God's presence with a heart to hear we will enjoy peace, hope, and joy.

Being with God brings healing of a yoked relationship even in life's darkest pain. This brings us to a place where we can understand the secrets of God that lead us to our breakthrough of spiritual wellness, divine healing and fully trusting in God.

"Divine healing comes when we name and recognize our suffering; this has to happen so we can move toward healing and draw strength from our pain. To deny our wounds is to miss the blessing God is creating out of our hardest times. To ignore our brokenness denies the miracles God can work to bring new life."[vii] We cannot move forward in our faith walk until we own where we are in this place called life. Faith follows the healing of our pain.

We cannot stay in our brokenness. We need to speak life in our situations and have total faith and trust in God. We should say to ourselves, this is the day of increased faith because I am in agreement to understand the secrets God has for me to live in divine healing of spiritual wellness.

We have faith to feel God's power and presence shifting in our lives. Whatever we believe, will happen. We will receive what we ask for. We take a close look at what God wants to do in our lives by developing our faith in the spirit of God.

In faith, we move forward in trusting what God has designed for us. God has provided a seed in us and it will manifest as we move in trusting relations with our faith in God. God loves us and we must trust God in leading us in our faith walk in being spiritually well. We have a seed of inspiration that God has placed in us that others need. Our lack of faith hinders God moving within our lives and the lives of those around us. We are not bound. We speak so that our seeds are blessed and our thoughts are blessed. Our faith will develop by the Spirit of God when we place ourselves in position to trust what God is speaking to us regarding all of our relationships.

Deuteronomy 6:5-6 (Common English Bible) states, "Love the Lord your God with all your heart, all your being, and all your strength. These words that I am commanding you today must always be on your minds." Our walk with God causes our love to grow stronger each day. When we love God with all our hearts, beings, and strengths, we give God everything within. Some of us have read and have recited this scripture many times. Have we tried applying our heart, being, and strength in our love towards God? By living this command, we connect with the plan God has designed for our lives.

Yes, I know some of us fall short in the area of fully loving God with all of our heart, being, and strength. Our love for God happens when we love others. We love and care for those whom God has given us to be in relationship with. When we are connected to the family of God, we begin to share, belong, serve, and suffer together. These connections build our love for God. By fellowshipping and worshiping together, we begin building genuine relationships with one another.

Our faith connects us to God's family. When we become whom God intends for us to be, we bring glory to God. Our trust in God helps us to stay in right relationship with others. This is why we must truly trust God and not anyone or anything else. People will let us down because they have their own expectations and oftentimes these expectations are not openly shared. This can end relationships. This is why we put our trust in God.

"Trust in the LORD with all your heart; don't rely on your own intelligence. Know God in all your paths, and God will keep your ways straight" (Proverbs 3:5-6, CEB). I remember hearing one of my seminary professors say, "If you hear something twice it must be important." In chapter one, we read and recite this passage of Proverbs 3:5-6 often, "Trust in the Lord." Life will show us why we should always keep our trust in God. We know God is the same yesterday, today, and forever (Hebrews 13:8). In all seasons, God remains the same.

As we rely on God's spirit, as Paul said, we will be guided in right relationships. I connect with God's spirit by trusting with my heart, mind, and strength. We will do well to remember Amos 3:3, "Will two people walk together unless they have agreed to do so?" In this text, the two walking together are God and Israel. When God brought Israel out of Egypt, a special relationship began and Israel became accountable to God's will. Though the people were sinful, God still had love for them. The prophet warned the people what was to come in hopes of giving them a chance to do right and walk together with God. There must be some type of agreement to walk together.

We must be mindful of our agreement to daily walk with God. Can we do it? Is it hard for us to stay in agreement in our walk with God? Like any other relationship, we have ups and downs. The same with our relationship with God, one day we are totally on board to do and be, with solid agreement about walking fully in our call. Other days, we miss the mark. We must renew and restore our minds daily with prayer and meditation to remember our agreement to follow the path that leads to spiritual wellness for our lives.

Use the journal lines on the next two pages to answer the following question.

How do you connect with God's Spirit?

Veronica Fallah

_____

_____

_____

_____

_____

_____

_____

_____

_____

_____

_____

_____

_____

Chapter Five:
Spouse

Can two people have a meaningful relationship without agreeing to do so? Marriage is a union designed to last until death. However, some commit to a union of marriage not knowing the challenges they will face.

I have also made commitments to love, honor, and obey in my marriages and at times these words were easier said than done.

I married my high school sweetheart on December 17,1988. I was young and fresh, ready for a long, loving relationship. We were both wet-behind-the ears, not knowing anything about a commitment to unite until death-do-us-part. We were just what we called "in love!"

My marriage required that I move to West Germany and the week before our wedding we met with the pastor of my church. He was so excited about our move overseas that he forgot to discuss the serious challenges a marital commitment would bring.

Everyone around us felt that what we had would work. We came from the same religion, race, and cultural settings. In our community's eyes, we looked like "a match made in heaven."

During my first marriage, we lived together four of the seven years we were married. From 1989 until 1992, we resided in West Germany. Some of our time apart was related to military assignments. In hindsight, I think what caused this marriage to end was a lack of communication and a lack of embracing the need to support one another.

When we returned to our hometown with our two daughters, our lack of agreeing to walk together was apparent in our familiar surroundings. I noticed that we had a better connection when we lived overseas, perhaps because we needed each other more during that time.

I recall one evening after work wanting to discuss some family plans. I shared goals I had in mind for us to build a home in our hometown and wanted to know if we were on the same page for our family life. Unfortunately, my former husband had checked out of our marriage way before I knew it and he did not have any goals in mind for our family life to move forward. In my attempt to invoke a unity of oneness within our marriage, I received an answer that left me feeling empty and alone. It was evident that we would not be one heart walking together as our hearts and minds were not connecting. This separateness went on for several months.

I took a vacation to visit my sister and her family in Oklahoma. My intent was to spend some time in prayer figuring out the path for my family's life. I knew my husband did not care if we were in town or not.

I often prayed for insight in my attempt to be a faithful wife, asking within my heart, "God give me insight of my future with this man." God placed a vision in my spiritual hearing. I heard in my spirit from the Lord that when I returned home, if my husband was home waiting for us to return, there was hope. If he was not at home, then we must part ways.

My daughters and I returned home to an empty house. There was no daddy for the girls to hug and no husband for me to kiss. That very day, I packed our bags and moved into my parent's home.

I wrestled with the thought of divorce, though I did not rush to get one. I reviewed scriptures and put all my human and spiritual energy into seeking God. I wanted to understand what this separation was going to mean for my daughters and me. Why was this relationship taking separate paths? We were from the same backgrounds. We should have been a "match made in heaven." However, we were not in agreement to walk the path of marriage together. Our relationship was not equally yoked. Just like the ox and the donkey, one was carrying more than the other and our balance was off.

After the divorce, I raised my daughters by myself and connected with my faith like never before. I was serving in my church community seven days a week. Whatever position needed to be filled, I found myself doing it. This serving kept me in the word of God, built my prayer life, and taught me how to fast more than twenty-four hours.

One winter evening in 2005, while in a local Wal-Mart getting tires for my car, a Middle Eastern guy began flirting with me and maybe all the other ladies shopping in the store that evening. When he asked for my phone number, I shared it with him and a few weeks later we connected and agreed to meet for dinner. After our first dinner date, we could not bear to be separated. We felt a connection of some type. It was like an unspoken agreement to continue to get to know one another. He mentioned during our first date that he wanted to join me for the evening service at my church. I declined his offer. Since the relationship was so new, I wanted to see where God was leading us.

Eventually, I did invite him to church, and we met each other's families. Many strangers and friends who take a narrow reading of "equally yoked" and do not look at the way God's Spirit yokes with each of us and then enables our relationships to participate in our spiritual wellness challenged me not to continue dating him. I chose to accept the gift God presented to me, to be this man's bride and he became my husband. Though the differences between us are great, I am very blessed. God's Spirit enables us to love with an open heart in spite of our differences.

My husband is of Iranian Turkish descent. I am African American. I was constantly asked again and again, "Are you equally yoked?" I asked several people to explain to me what that meant. They would say things like, "Same religion, race, and/or cultural/ethnic backgrounds." What they meant was did we share the same similarities and commonalities. You may be shaking your head in agreement with their statements. However, what I was experiencing in my relationship with my present husband Kia was different than what I had experienced in any of my previous relationships that were supposedly, "equally yoked." In previous relationships, it had been challenging to agree to walk together. In my present marriage, two of our main strengths are communication and support for one another. We openly communicate to figure out the paths we wish to walk together.

I am not saying that we do not experience challenges, but there is no guessing about what we are looking for. We talk, we support and we wrestle through the challenges of blending our beliefs while raising daughters and grandchildren. We have learned to work through these challenges openly sharing the good, bad, and indifferent. As stated in Amos 3:3, "Will two people walk together unless they have agreed to do so?" Our support for one another is better than what I have had in any relationship besides my relationship with God.

Kia comes with his traditions and I have mine. We choose to put them before us and figure out the best plan for our family situation and ourselves. I am most grateful to God in showing us how to work together to bring the balance that is needed in our marriage and I pray that what we have had in these ten years of applying the fruit of the spirit - love, joy, peace, patience, kindness, goodness, faithfulness, gentleness and self-control - as stated in Galatians 5:22-23, will continue to lead us on a path of "holy matrimony" with all of our differences.

The main thing I have learned concerning my marriage is to trust the Spirit of God in all things. We should not allow traditions to trap us in a plan that God has not designed for us. God wants to use us as examples of His plan working in our lives to bring wellness not only for us but also those God has placed in our lives.

You may not agree with what a union of marriage means to me. But, I have learned to embrace God's Spirit within and welcome diversity into my own life. Just as our world is "a beautiful mosaic: different people, different beliefs, different yearnings, different hopes, and different dreams,"[viii] so is my marriage with my husband. It works for us. And our coming together has given us a wealth of knowledge we would have not gained if we did not embrace the love of God in each other. Your connection to agree to walk with another may differ. We must hold fast to our own convictions and live our lives of spiritual wellness in each of our own marriages.

I pray that you come to your own conclusion in what equally yoked in marriage means to you. My prayer is that you connect with the Spirit of God to find what gives your marriage that trust for spiritual wellness. What are your values and beliefs that yoke you to live your best in a marital relationship?

Do you believe if persons are from the same religion, race, and cultural setting they are equally yoked? Are they really in agreement to walk a path together? Do those things alone guarantee a successful marriage?

In my experience, this walking in agreement is deeper than having the same background. It's a move only connected by the Spirit of God within. And, both people in the relationship must have a place where they can be still and know the path God wants to lead them on in this world of diversity.

In a too-busy world, people *cannot* have a connection to the Spirit of God. We must take time to BE STILL. Psalm 46:10, "Be still and know." If two people take time out of their busy schedule and pray together, the Spirit can yoke them even if everything else about them is different. In a marriage relationship, the couple must find that balance in which they are yoked. If they are together in the Spirit, the Spirit makes up the difference, or the Spirit creates a unique yoke that enables these two people to pull together.

When it comes to choosing or committing to walk our life's path with another, we must connect to the Spirit within for a deeper connection than commonality. In some cases, commonality works perfectly. However for my life's path, in my first marriage, this commonality of race, religion, and cultural setting brought us to a crossroad that led us toward separate paths. In my second marriage, connecting to diversity and God's Spirit has led us on a path of agreeing to walk together. We continue to learn how to honor and respect one another. We have listened to the need and with the help of God's Spirit within us, we hear one another and have agreed to walk the path ahead together.

The main thing I have learned concerning my marriage is to trust the Spirit of God in all things. We should not allow traditions to trap us in a plan that God has not designed for us. God wants to use us as examples of His plan working in our lives to bring wellness not only for us but also those God has placed in our lives.

Use the journal lines on the next few pages to answer the following question.

What is your agreement with your companion?

_____

_____

_____

_____

_____

_____

_____

_____

_____

_____

_____

_____

_____

_____

_____

_____

_____

_____

_____

_____

_____

_____

_____

_____

_____

Chapter Six:
Family Circle

In my family structure, I am what my family called the "knee-baby." While my baby brother was in my parent's arms, I was old enough to be held on their knees. I grew up in what was considered a traditional two-parent household with three older siblings, my baby brother and I. Dad went to work and Mom raised the children. When hard times hit, my mom had to work outside the home as well to help make ends meet.

I believe we had structure within our family circle and we were yoked together at times and at other times we were not yoked. It is all part of a family moving toward a goal of connecting to a relationship and trust for spiritual wellness in being equally yoked.

I say we had the yoked part right at times and not at others due to the ups and downs in the family household. Being in a household with siblings, tension happened among us. I recall being the one who always received discipline when something happened in our family and my parents did not spare the rod. They used it faithfully.

My parents raised us in the Christian faith by teaching us prayers, scriptures, and the love of God. We also attended weekly church services. Our family roots were and still are deeply connected to biblical teachings. My parents served faithfully in their church and from their faithful service they birthed a youth director, an elder, chaplain, and a pastor. Some of their grandchildren are also choosing to serve in some ministerial capacity. And, even though there is much ministry in my family, we still have a ways to go before becoming equally yoked and connecting to the relationship and trust for spiritual wellness. This is an observation of my family as a whole.

I am one who likes the support and interaction of family gatherings and do what I can to actively show all of my family members (immediate and extended) that my husband and I are here for them. However, this interaction is not always appreciated, as much as I would like.

I recall gathering during one of our annual family reunions. My cousins and I had worked diligently to design an engaging reunion for all of our relatives. However, some of the family members were not appreciative of our service of love and flat out rejected what we had to offer, choosing not to participate in the weekend festivities. I was disappointed in their decision to not join us since most of the family who attended had traveled to be with them in our hometown.

I cannot continue to pour out when it seems like the giving or the connecting is not accepted by some of my family members. When I notice the lack in accepting an invite to connect, it changes the relationship between my family member and I. I am sure some of us have felt at some point in our family relationships that our family members do not value what is brought to assist in building together.

We must take time to nurture the families God has given us. We are not going to agree all the time. However, when a family member reaches out to us with a concern or we notice a problem within our immediate or extended family circle, I believe it is our duty to go and restore that member as it is stated throughout our biblical readings.

Family structure can be complex and life happens: the good, bad, and indifferent. There are not many family households that are free from life's challenges. Whatever the challenges may be within our family units, we must bind our forces together and restore each other. I believe families should have a continuous line of communication. This should not happen only during special occasions. There should be a continuation of building a strong family bond that leads to being equally yoked and living toward relationship and trust for spiritual wellness within each family unit.

Is your family equally yoked? Does your family have a strong structure of support in every area of life? What does your family agreement look like with your immediate and extended family?

Use the journal lines on the next two pages to answer the questions above.

Chapter Seven:
Friendships

Within the context of friendship, I have learned to love people where they were and move on when the plowing on the paths to these friends became unbalanced. Remember the scripture Amos 3:3, "Will two people walk together unless they have agreed to do so?" I have been blessed to be in relationships with good friends. In elementary school, I met friends that I still connect with. Sometimes our relationships are stronger than at other times, but I still call these people my friends.

In elementary school, there was a girl who acted like a little dictator. She told us who to like and who not to like in order to stay connected to the popular group in school. Each week there was a different kid we were told not to like. This little girl was never on the end of not being liked. One day, a new girl started going to our school and she noticed this little dictator was giving our classmates orders to not like her. The new girl questioned the little dictator and questioned the rest of us as to why we continued to allow her to tell us who to like or who not to like. The new girl, now my friend, gave this little dictator a taste of her own medicine. From that day forward, the little dictator no longer controlled her classmates and the students began to build true friendships on their own.

As time went on, I developed friendships in my neighborhood, at school, at work, and at church. Each of these relationships gave me what I needed in a friend. And through these relationships, I learned what I appreciated and what I did not.

What I have observed about myself is that I desire long lasting friendships and I take the ending of relationships very hard. I never want to let go and I am always reaching out to see how I can rekindle relationships with friends I have had. God has taught me to love people where they are and that sometimes I have to move on. We have to decide if we can continue on the same path or if it's time for some friendships to go their separate ways. The crossroads in a friendship are a struggle and the friends in the relationship must walk in their truth that leads each to being spiritually well.

Friends come and go in our lives; some are for a lifetime and others are for a season. Throughout my connection with friends, I have experienced genuine friendships and in others, just relationships to get what they needed.

Within friendships, seasons do change. Schoolmates grow up and move on. People change jobs. People move from the neighborhood and church membership changes. All of these situations caused an end to many of my relationships.

During the time when I was a single mom, God led numerous women into my immediate circle. I believe we each had strengths to support each other in being equally yoked in our own relationship. It seemed like there was not a day that went by without being in an active relationship with one another.

Our fellowship and support for one another with our children allowed us to depend on each other. Being forthright and honesty was the glue that allowed our relationships to last during that season of our lives.

Transparency in my friendships means my friends know exactly whom they are with at all times. I share with complete honesty in building friendships with whoever accepts the invitation of my friendship. I believe that in being transparent, I have helped others and have encouraged them to be transparent as well.

I have had joys and disappointments in friendships. I also noticed some friends were not true and open to me. Poet and author Maya Angelou said, "When someone shows you who they are, believe them the first time." If we are in a friendship long enough, we should be able to see if it is going to last or count it as an experience of the past. Not everyone we meet is meant to stay in our lives forever. Some are there for a season and at times it is hard to embrace a new season in life due to being comfortable in the season we are presently in. God knows what or whom we need and when we need it or them. And when the need is met, God moves or closes the chapter and starts a new one in our lives.

Are we equally yoked in our friendships? Do we pour out our feelings to the pseudo social media friends or are we connected in true friendships? What are the expectations agreed on in a friendship? Is the plowing on the paths to our friendships balanced?

Use the journal lines on the next two pages to answer the questions above.

_____

_____

_____

_____

_____

_____

_____

_____

_____

_____

_____

_____

Chapter Eight:
Vocations

I have worked since the age of sixteen. I learned at an early age to grow in the vocation in which I am called to serve. In the past three years, I have experienced company closings. When two of the companies I worked for closed, this led me to explore being called to my vocation in another light.

I asked myself if I was the common denominator in the closings. I believe God was leading me to explore the gifts and talents within me. I asked myself if God was telling me to use what He had created within me to live a sustainable life in serving others as an entrepreneur.

I recalled my parents sharing with me that they wanted me to complete high school and find myself a "good job." I completed high school and God strengthened me to complete my Bachelor of Social Psychology and my Masters in Divinity. My educational route was a non-traditional one. I started my first year in college six years after high school, as a married woman with two daughters. I believe God yoked me in my studies to complete all of the tasks that were set before me.

I had followed both of my parents' advice and completed high school and went into the "workforce." I had many entry-level and professional positions and I had worked my best in every area. Were those positions my "yoked" vocations? I can definitely say those positions were all learning experiences in which I gained a greater understanding in what it means to be equally yoked with one's vocation.

I prayed and pondered before studying to become a chaplain. When I felt this was where I was being led, I started the journey. This "road less traveled" journey took me eleven years to complete. But in order to be equally yoked in the vocation God was leading me, I listened to the voice of God compelling me to answer my call to chaplaincy. Listening is one of my spiritual gifts. Have you heard your call to fortify your spiritual gift? Your spiritual gifts may be your yoked place for a vocation that gives your life meaning and purpose.

While he was in prison, Paul wrote his letter to the church in Ephesus to strengthen their congregation. He wanted them to understand their spiritual reality by encouraging them in their faith walk, while each of them learned how to walk in unity using their own spiritual gifts. "The Ephesians church was commended for hearing Paul and not tolerating false teachers; however, they needed to recapture their first love for God."ix Paul's message to the Christians of Ephesus was a call to connect to their love for God. "Therefore, as a prisoner for the Lord, I encourage you to live as people worthy of the call you received from God. Conduct yourselves with all humility, gentleness, and patience. Accept each other with love, and make an effort to preserve the unity of the Spirit with the peace that ties you together" (Ephesians 4:1-3).

To walk worthy of the call received from God, each believer's life should match the excellences of Christ's calling. Christ lived a life of humbleness, gentleness and longsuffering. Some might say, "That is Christ. I do not know if I can walk in my call with others humbly or gently and, God knows, longsuffering is way too much!"

However, we must not worry. If we keep our focus as Paul tells us, "We can do all things through Christ who strengthens us" (Philippians 4:13). This is a call to believe. When we build our walk of faith in Christ, Christ's spirit will empower us to consistently treat people in a humble, gentle, and patient way. We each have our own spiritual gifts that edify the body of Christ and the community we live in.

My gift happens to be in the area of Spiritual Wellness. Though I did not know how to name it as a child, my call to chaplaincy began developing at a young age. I remember being a preteen sitting with bedridden people. I read scriptures to them and we prayed and sang songs with them. I did not know what God had placed in my heart as a child would be my service to the world today.

In the early 1990s, I worked for a local hospital as a Care Assistant. At that time, my aspiration was to become a nurse. Unfortunately, one of our hemophilia patients died in the clinic. The medical staff was at a loss in knowing how to care for the spiritual needs of the family who had just lost their young child and asked me to sit with the family members until they could find a chaplain to be with them.

Sometimes your call will come in unexpected ways. Are you open to hearing the call on your life? You may ask, how do I know for sure what my call is? Trust the process. We receive validation from the Spirit of God when we allow our values and beliefs to connect with our actions. Our call is in the realm that gives our life meaning and purpose.

Those skills God developed within me as a child began to flow in the room with the family members during their painful loss. God allowed genuine empathy and gentleness to fill the room as the family reached toward me with open arms and allowed me to embrace them. As we hugged, the family members of the deceased child shared about their loved one and I listened with empathy and compassion.

God has equipped me with a heart to see and hear how to embrace all of God's people in a way that would lead them to spiritual wellness. We often hear about and see healthcare workers who focus on physical, medical, mental, and behavioral wellness. However, spiritual wellness is not always addressed. As the Spiritual Wellness Pastor at PowerShift Worship Center and the owner of Venerate Care, my goal is to help others fortify their own spiritual wellness by helping them become centered to hear God's voice and to live by their values and beliefs for their own wellness.

Spiritual Wellness is a non-traditional ministry that supports people outside of the four walls of their faith or non-faith communities. The ministry builds a bridge between other faith groups so that each religious practice can work towards the common goal of the community. No matter what the community is, we share a common humanity — and to be human is to be *ethical* and to be *spiritual.* We cannot be well and whole without nurturing our ethical and spiritual core.

I have a mission to provide emotional and spiritual support for all people. This support includes providing non-judgmental pastoral counseling and support, and assessing their spiritual and religious needs. I hear their concept of God and meaning of their illness and in some cases imminent death. It is important to talk with patients about their approach to hope and their relationships with their support system. I also provide prayer, if requested.

As a Spiritual Wellness Pastor, I strongly connect to PowerShift Worship Center's mission which is to "love God, transform lives and communities, and impact the world" with my spiritual gift in serving those where they are in their own life's journey. To me, the one-on-one ministry has a great impact in helping people walk a life path worthy of the call to their vocation and living spiritually well.

My call in this vocation of chaplaincy is rigorous and it is a call I do not take lightly. I enjoy the full process of providing care as a chaplain as well as being cared for by other chaplains when I am dealing with life's concerns. I truly believe that in order to lead we must be willing to follow. I know some chaplains who do not agree to get care as I would.

My journey with these types of chaplains opened my eyes to different reasons why others may enter a vocation. It also causes the words of my father to echo in my mind, "Trust no man." We never know the motives of some people. However, serving as a chaplain is most rewarding to me. I enjoy serving so much I often volunteer as a chaplain. I feel equally yoked in this vocation as a servant of the gospel. Whatever vocation we are called to do, be open to learn from others.

I have worked in the healthcare industry and in Christian ministry most of my life and I can tell you, I have felt the growing pains in serving in areas which God has stamped with completion. When God's Spirit prompts us to move to the next chapter, embrace it and we will see God develop great things with our gifts and talents. We will know when we are truly in our called vocation because we will serve in it without compensation. It will be our yoked placed of wellness.

Are you equally yoked in your vocation? Do you connect with trust and relationship for spiritual wellness as you serve in the areas you believe God has called you to serve? When you face rejection in your called vocation, how do you stand in wellness to continue to serve in that area?

Use the journal lines on the next two pages to answer the questions above.

_____

_____

_____

_____

_____

_____

_____

_____

_____

_____

_____

_____

Chapter Nine:
In Our Faith Communities

In her song *No Pain, No Gain,* soul singer, Betty Wright sings, "if you learn this secret, how to forgive, a longer and better life you'll live... in order to get something you got to go through something... no pain, no gain."[x] This song refers to a relationship between a man and a woman, though the lyrics can connect to any type of relationship — even relationships within our faith communities. Can we be equally yoked with the love of God in our fellowship while experiencing ups and downs within our faith community at the same time?

Sometimes in the faith community there are hurts and pain. I feel that "church hurt" — pain from our family of faith — is the most painful hurt we can endure. We must continue to gather together in fellowship to overcome the pain and to enjoy the gain. Hebrews 10:25 encourages us, "not forsaking the assembling of ourselves together, as *is* the manner of some, but exhorting *one another*...."[xi] Our gathering in our faith communities builds our faith in God, one another, as well as helps us to embrace a path of yoked (easy) relationships. Can we grow from our hurt and pain that happens within our faith communities?

During my life, I have had the opportunity to worship and fellowship with Christians as well as other faith traditions. I have enjoyed the common ground of plowing together within my faith community including the ups and the downs. The smooth and bumpy experiences while serving and worshiping within the faith community have developed my faith in a love relationship to continue to serve at all times.

While I was a young woman living in West Germany, I worshiped with the Church of God in Christ. I was appointed to lead the "Young Women Christian Council," a women's ministry for women under forty. I was so excited to work with the members in this ministry. I brought to the position everything I had learned about serving in the ministry. However, not everyone accepted what I had to offer. Even back then, I had a heart for people. My compassion for the people of God and willingness to step in an assist where needed rubbed some of the people the wrong way. Some of the leaders believed I did not look the part to lead the "Young Women Christian Council," and attempted to groom me into the person they thought I should be on the outside. I remember being told to take off my earrings, remove my make-up, and to not wear long pants. To me there was too much emphasis on the outer appearance. I felt all of these restrictions on the outer appearance limited what was important for my soul.

One year, the pastor appointed me to lead the pastor's appreciation service, but some of the members did not agree with the pastor's decision. Every idea I suggested was thumbed down and when I asked for input, members kept quiet. It was a losing battle. It felt like the whole committee was out to ambush me, something akin to a deer stunned by headlights. The pain of rejection within my faith community hurt me.

I prayed to God for comfort and God reminded me that my agreement to lead the appreciation service was with God and the pastor. And with their agreement, the vision within came to life. I yoked myself with the strength within. The members connected with the vision, and we moved forward with the appreciation service. God moved. People's lives were changed, and I learned to hold fast to my faith within and love the people of God where they were.

Years went by and I found myself working diligently with another faith community for over fourteen years. Who would have known I was going to face another hurtful encounter within the community of faith? In 2001, the church members had scheduled a cruise. Unfortunately 9/11 happened and members were afraid to travel. A friend, who happened to be the pastor's relative, and I decided we would continue with our plans to cruise. The pastor's wife came to me in a very unloving way and said, "I do not care what you plan to do, but my relative will not be joining you on a cruise." I was stunned and deeply hurt by the comment and wondered why the pastor's wife was not concerned about me as a member of the same community of faith.

In some of our faith communities, we have leaders in place who are unaware of how their actions can hurt a member who may look up to them for direction. Just as Jesus's own rejected him, I guess we as followers are going to experience some of these same rejections by members of our own community of faith.

How does one connect to God's Spirit while being rejected by members of their own faith community? For me, prayer gives me the peace to carry on. This prayer by St. Francis connects me with trust for spiritual wellness.

A Simple Prayer
Attributed to St. Francis of Assisi
1181-1226 A.D.

Lord, make me an instrument of your peace,
Where there is hatred, let me sow love;
Where there is injury, pardon;
Where there is doubt, faith;
Where there is despair, hope;
Where there is darkness, light;
Where there is sadness, joy;

O Divine Master, grant that I may not so much
seek to be consoled as to console;
To be understood as to understand;
To be loved as to love.

For it is in giving that we receive;
It is in pardoning that we are pardoned;
And it is in dying that we are born to eternal life.[xii]

Prayer and scripture keep me on the path of being equally yoked to God's Spirit, which blesses me with the spiritual health to trust God. Yoked with God's Spirit, I can enter into relationships, even very different ones, with the strength and discernment to love others even when they do not demonstrate love to me. Paul writes in Romans 8:28; 33-37, "And we know that all things work together for good to those who love God, to those who are the called according to His purpose...Who shall bring a charge against God's elect? It is God who justifies. Who is he who condemns...Shall tribulation, or distress, or persecution, or famine, or nakedness, or peril, or sword? As it is written: "For Your sake we are killed all day long: We are accounted as sheep for the slaughter." Yet in all these things we are more than conquerors through Him who loved us."[xiii]

God's love leads us on our journeys of being yoked and teaches us how to love while going through hurt and pain. Reading and reflecting on the word of God will give us peace in the midst of being judged unjustly.

Is it possible to love while we are being persecuted? Are we truly living lives of love? Is the hurt and pain in our lives keeping us from loving with the love of God?

People will let us know how they feel about us by their actions. We should ignore the words and watch their actions. In each of the ministry settings that I have worshipped, I have had some type of hurtful and painful interaction. How should we handle the hurt and pain within our faith community? Where is God calling us when we face challenges in our fellowship? Do we connect to our faith that leads us to peace and love? Thinking of the word relationship when it comes to being equally yoked, are we equally yoked in our communities of faith?

God has called us to share, belong, serve, and suffer together. We hear messages that encourage us to live in right relationship with one another while we are doing all we can to work together for the greater good of our connected communities. This corporate worship is designed for us to bind our cords together in unity to be led on a path of being equally yoked in trust and relationship for spiritual wellness.

Use the journal lines on the next few pages to answer the following question.

What yokes you to your faith community?

_____

_____

_____

_____

_____

_____

_____

_____

_____

_____

_____

_____

_____

_____

_____

_____

_____

_____

_____

_____

_____

_____

_____

_____

_____

_____

_____

_____

_____

_____

_____

_____

_____

_____

_____

_____

_____

_____

_____

Conclusion

In life, we must know that we are going to have waves in our relationship; some are going to be high and others low. However, we must know what we bring to each of our interactions with God, others, and ourselves. *Equally Yoked: Trust and Relationship For Spiritual Wellness* has been written to help those who desire an understanding of what equally yoked and walking in an agreement means to them. In this place called "life," we must learn to connect with the power of God within, trusting and believing God's direction for our paths of life. We have read in this book about relationships and know that there are differences in our world. Are we open to connect to the diversity that the world has? God is calling us to unity, peace and love. We know in our hearts that if we do not connect to unity, peace, and love, there can be no spiritual wellness.

Have we connected to the spirit within or do we look for others to validate what God has already approved for us? Are we open to connect with the differences within the world in our faith community? Can two really walk together in agreement in a world of differences? What does equally yoked mean to us within our faith community?

We have journeyed through these chapters in reflection of being equally yoked in relationships of trust that lead to spiritual wellness with God; spouse; family; friends; vocations; and community of faith. We used many scriptures and highlighted Amos 3:3, "Will two people walk together unless they have agreed to do so." The answer is in our daily walk of commitments in how we choose to fortify our own spiritual lives. *Do we honestly connect to our values and beliefs? Do we live in a realm that gives our life meaning and purpose?* If we can answer yes, then we are living spiritually well.

Use the journal lines on the next two pages to answer the questions above and to write down your thoughts about being "equally yoked" after having completed this book.

Veronica Fallah

_____

_____

_____

_____

_____

_____

_____

_____

_____

_____

_____

_____

_____

I have known Reverend Veronica Fallah long enough to realize what a wonderful gift she is to those who have met her. She is a friend, a sister in Christ, a spiritual counselor, and one of the best listeners I know. She works tirelessly serving as the Associate Minister of PowerShift Worship Center in Raytown, Missouri, as a Chaplain, as the founder of Venerate Care, LLC, and as the Disciples of Christ Women's Transitional Coordinator in the Greater Kansas City region.

Chaplain Fallah has certainly interacted with many people. I think this qualifies her to write about people being equally yoked in all phases of their lives. In this book, Chaplain Fallah gives us a fresh and different look at relationships, which include: our families, jobs, friendships, marriages and partnerships, and in our faith communities.

If you are looking for a wise perspective on living life more equal, this book can be your guide.

Mae Thomas
PowerShift Worship Center CCDOC
Care and Compassion Minister
Children's Church Leader

We must learn to trust God's spirit within while building trusting relationships with each other.

The main thing I have learned concerning my marriages is to trust the spirit of God in all things. We should not allow traditions to trap us in a plan that God has not designed for us. God wants to use us as examples of God's plans working in our lives that not only brings wellness for us but also those God has placed in our lives.

What is it that brings us to an agreement with another person? Are our expectations, spoken and unspoken, made clear in our agreements to walk together? Journey with me on the development of being "equally yoked" and embrace the trust and relationships God gives you for spiritual wellness.

Connect with Chaplain Veronica at:
www.veronicafallah.com

Chaplain Veronica Fallah

Owner
Venerate Care, LLC

Pastoral Care Pastor
at PowerShift
Worship Center
Christian Church
(DOC)

Local Hospital
Chaplain

Veronica Fallah serves as the Disciples Women Ministry Transitional Coordinator, owner of Venerate Care, a local hospital Chaplain, and an associate Pastor at PowerShift Worship Center. She has more than 20 years of healthcare and ministry experience, which led her to create a spiritual & life wellness service to aid others with (w)holistic care by providing nurturing support to one's mind, body, and soul. With having a desire to see "all live spiritually well through their own faith journey... in the midst of their life challenges." Veronica currently resides in Kansas City, Missouri with her husband.

Endnotes:

i John Gill's exposition of the Bible [online] http://biblehub.com/commentaries/deuterono my/22-10.htm   (2016)

ii Jimmy Carter, *President* [online] www.president/jimmycarter (2016)

iii *A Disciples of Christ Pro-Reconciliation Anti-Racism* training in the Kansas City Regional Meeting (2014)

iv New International Version (Study Bible notes on Psalm 37,) pg. 914

v Herbert Lockyer, *All the Women of the Bible* (Grand Rapids, Michigan: Zondervan, 1967) pg. 165

vi New International Version Bible, 1 Corinthians 2:4, 5, 9

vii Susan Sonnenday Vogel, *What about Divine Healing* (Nashville, Tennessee: Abingdon Press, 2004) pg. 76

viii Jimmy Carter, *President* [online] www.president/jimmycarter (2016)
ix New King James Version Bible, (Study Bible Notes) Pg. 1981

x Betty Wright, Lyrics to *No Pain, No Gain* [online] www.azlyrics.com (2016)

xi New King James Version Bible, Hebrews 10:25

xii www.catholic.org Make me an Instrument of your Peace, Prayer of St. Francis of Assisi

xiii New King James Version Bible, Romans 8:28; 33-37

www.ingramcontent.com/pod-product-compliance
Lightning Source LLC
LaVergne TN
LVHW051701080426
835511LV00017B/2661